# CRITICAL PLANT LIFE

## BY VALERIE BODDEN

CREATIVE EDUCATION

Published by Creative Education
P.O. Box 227, Mankato, Minnesota 56002
Creative Education is an imprint of
The Creative Company
www.thecreativecompany.us

Design and production by The Design Lab
Art direction by Rita Marshall
Printed by Corporate Graphics in the
United States of America

Photographs by Alamy (The Garden Picture
Library, Imagebroker, Tim Manley/Cen-
tral America, Oaktree Photographic, Photo
Resource Hawaii, PVstock.com), iStockphoto
(Xavi Arnau, Anthony Brown, Dennis Burns,
Marcus Clackson, Giorgio Fochesato, Eric
Foltz, Alexander Hafemann, Stephen Inglis,
Lawrence Karn, Danish Khan, James Knight-
en, Nancy Louie, Mayumi Terao)

Library of Congress
Cataloging-in-Publication Data
Bodden, Valerie.
Critical plant life / by Valerie Bodden.
p. cm. — (Earth issues)
Includes bibliographical references and index.
Summary: An examination of the endanger-
ment and extinction of certain plant life,
exploring how plants in general affect Earth's
biodiversity and temperature, as well as how
they contribute to a healthier planet.
ISBN 978-1-58341-984-7
1. Plant ecophysiology—Juvenile literature. 2.
Plant ecology—Juvenile literature. 3. Plants—
Environmental aspects—Juvenile literature. 4.
Endangered plants—Juvenile literature. I. Title.
II. Series.

QK717.B63 2010
581.7—dc22          2009028047

CPSIA: 120109 PO1091
First Edition
9 8 7 6 5 4 3 2 1

# Table of Contents

Everything human beings need to survive—air to breathe, food to eat, water to drink—is found on Earth, and on Earth alone. Yet the very planet that sustains human life has come under threat because of human activities. Rivers are drying up as people divert water for their own use. Temperatures are warming as greenhouse gases such as carbon dioxide trap heat in the **atmosphere**. Species of plants and animals are disappearing as people destroy essential habitats. And the rate of many such changes appears to be accelerating. "If I had to use one word to describe the environmental state of the planet right now, I think I would say precarious," said population expert Robert Engelman. "It isn't doomed. It isn't certainly headed toward disaster. But it's in a very precarious situation right now."

Among the many problems that Earth's environment faces, the endangerment and extinction of plants doesn't always receive a lot of attention. Endangered plants often aren't as fascinating or as visible as threatened animals such as tigers or pandas. The loss of plants doesn't sound as alarming as the gradual warming of the planet. But the

Earth's other environmental issues, affecting both the planet's **biodiversity** and its temperature, along with the quality of life—and survival—of human beings. But why are plants disappearing? And how does the loss of an obscure tropical tree or a rare cactus affect people's lives? Is there anything we can do to prevent plants from becom-

Plants are the only organisms on the earth (apart from some bacteria) that have the ability to produce their own food through a process known as photosynthesis. Photosynthesis occurs in tiny structures in plant leaves and stems called chloroplasts, which contain a **pigment** called chlorophyll that absorbs light from the sun and makes plants green. Sunlight provides the energy plants need to combine the carbon dioxide absorbed from the atmosphere with water drawn up from the soil to produce sugars. In the process, water **molecules** are chemically split into their component elements—hydrogen and oxygen—and oxygen is released into the atmosphere as a waste product. Much of the water that plants draw up through their roots is not used in the process of photosynthesis and is released back into the air in its gaseous form as water vapor through a process called transpiration.

CHAPTER ONE

# Growing Green

A great diversity of plant species populates the earth. To date, scientists have identified about 288,000 species of plants, but every year, about 2,000 previously unidentified species of plants are discovered, leading some to estimate that the total number of plant species on Earth may be much higher. Some scientists put the figure as high as 422,000 to 472,000 when as-yet undiscovered species are taken into account.

Flowering plants, or angiosperms, are the most abundant plants on Earth, making up 80 to 90 percent of all plant life. Angiosperms are characterized by seeds that have a shell-like coating. Flowering plant species include most shrubs and herbs, many tree species (aside from conifers and other cone-bearing trees), **succulents**, and most food plants, including rice and corn. Conifers belong to a different group of plants that produce seed-bearing cones. All but 15 or so

Succulent flowering plants such as cholla cacti are found throughout the dry regions of Mexico and the American Southwest.

Mosses thrive in damp, shaded areas, making a secluded forest floor an ideal location to find the carpets of flowerless green plants.

of the world's 550 species of conifer are evergreen. Like most conifers, plants belonging to the cycad group are evergreen and reproduce through cones, but while many conifers look like pine trees, most cycads look somewhat like palm trees. Most of the 300-some cycad species can be found in the tropics and subtropics. Other groups of plants include ferns, horsetails, and club mosses. Bryophytes are the simplest plants. They include 18,000 to 25,000 species of mosses, liverworts, and hornworts.

Plants can be found almost everywhere on Earth. In fact, plants make up about 90 percent of the total biomass (weight of living organisms) of most **ecosystems**, and, in general, the world's

**biomes** are classified on the basis of the dominant plants that live within them. Forest biomes, for example, are dominated by trees, whether they be the conifers that thrive in **boreal** forests or the **deciduous** trees that cover **temperate** forests. The tropical rainforests are a hotbed of plant diversity, containing about 67 percent of all plant species on Earth. In the Amazon rainforest of Brazil, as many as 120 different plant species can grow on a single acre (0.4 ha) of land.

Like rainforests, Mediterranean biomes, which are characterized by cool, rainy winters and warm, dry summers, are home to a wide array of plants. Mediterranean biomes are found in five parts of

Aspen is a species of deciduous tree known for the brilliancy of its leaf colors in the fall, and its bark is a food source for some butterflies.

## Greener Pastures

Humans are not the only creatures affected by the loss of plant species. Plants serve as a food source and habitat for countless animals, and every time a plant species becomes extinct, or dies out, as many as 30 other animal (and plant) species may be reduced. In fact, 75 percent of endangered **mammals**, including orangutans and pandas, are threatened by the loss of forests. Animals that rely exclusively on one plant species for food, habitat, or reproduction are especially at risk. The Karner blue butterfly, for example, lays its eggs only on blue wild lupine. If this plant were to become extinct, so would the butterfly.

the world: the coastal areas of the Mediterranean Sea, much of California, central Chile, the tip of South Africa, and southwestern Australia. They cover only 1 to 2 percent of Earth's land surface but contain 20 percent of the world's plant species. In fact, the Cape Floristic Region in South Africa hosts more species of plants per acre (0.4 ha) than does the Amazon rainforest.

With a semi-arid climate, grassland biomes differ from both forests and Mediterranean regions. As the name implies, grasslands are dominated by grasses and wildflowers. The world's temperate grasslands include the prairies of North America, the pampas of South America, and the steppes of Europe and Asia. The savannas of Africa, Australia, and South America are the most extensive grasslands of all, accounting for 75 percent of all grassland biomes. Savannas in tropical regions often have a short rainy season, which allows them to support scattered trees. Deserts, on the other hand, are characterized by little to no rainfall, so the plants that grow in desert biomes are adapted to conserve water. Although cacti and ground-hugging shrubs form the majority of a desert's plant life, some deserts bloom with bright wildflowers after a rainfall.

With so many different plants growing in such a wide variety of locations—many of which are quite remote—it can be difficult for scientists to determine the number of plant species at risk of extinction. The most authoritative source for endangered plant species is the Red List of Threatened Species, updated annually by the International Union for Conservation of Nature (IUCN). The 2008 IUCN Red List evaluated a total of about 12,000 plant species, which represents about 4 percent of all known plants. Of the species assessed, 115 were either completely extinct or extinct in the wild, while nearly 8,460 were classified as critically endangered, endangered, or vulnerable to extinction. Some species are

The introduction of grazing cattle caused much damage to the habitat of Clay's hibiscus, leaving it vulnerable to animals and encroaching weeds.

so close to extinction—with only a few surviving individuals—that they are known as the "living dead." Among them is the Clay's hibiscus, a tree native to the Hawaiian island of Kauai, of which only four individual specimens remain in the wild.

Like the Clay's hibiscus, many of the world's most threatened plant species are endemic, meaning that their growth is restricted to a specific geographic region, such as an island or mountain. The areas of the world with the highest levels of endemism include the islands of Madagascar, New Caledonia, and Hawaii, as well as parts of Brazil and South Africa. In fact, 69 percent of the plant species in South Africa's Cape Floristic Region can be found nowhere else on Earth. Today, 618 plant species from this region are at risk of extinction, and 36 have already permanently disappeared from the planet.

Earth's 6.8 billion inhabitants have made a major impact on the planet's natural environment. To date, humans have altered half of all land area on Earth, making habitat destruction one of the leading causes of plant endangerment, along with **overexploitation**, invasive species of plants and pests, pollution, and global warming. Of all causes, habitat destruction is the most deadly to plant populations, imperiling 85 percent of all endangered plant species. One of the most visible causes of plant habitat destruction is apparent in the logging of the world's forests. According to some estimates, 50 to 75 percent of all the earth's forested lands have already been cleared, and in some parts of the world—such as Nigeria, China, Vietnam, Guatemala, Sweden, and the United States—at least 90 percent of native forestland is gone. Although temperate forests are today beginning to see an increase in area as once-cleared lands are replanted, tropical forests continue to lose about 32 million acres (13 million ha) each year, or about 50 football-field-sized segments every minute.

CHAPTER TWO

# Pressures on Plants

Fast-growing conifers, with their straight trunks, account for 70 percent of commercially logged wood, but **hardwoods** such as mahogany and teak are not without threat. Many of these trees are rare and slow-growing, making them both incredibly valuable and vulnerable to extinction. In many parts of the world, logging of these species is illegal, but this rarely stops loggers, who can make a small fortune on the sale of a single tree. In the Amazon rainforest of Brazil, 60 percent of logging is carried out illegally.

Logging for timber is not the only cause of deforestation. Often, trees are cleared from the land in order to create room for farming. In the tropics, the use of former forestland for agricul-

The destruction of forests affects all the species that call that particular habitat home, from small plants and insects to larger creatures.

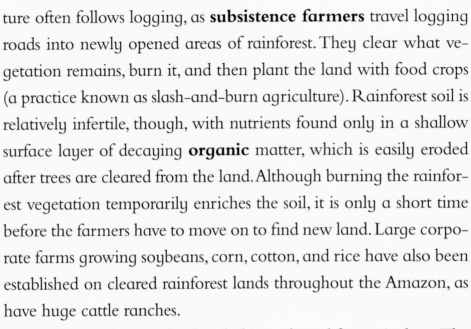

ture often follows logging, as **subsistence farmers** travel logging roads into newly opened areas of rainforest. They clear what vegetation remains, burn it, and then plant the land with food crops (a practice known as slash-and-burn agriculture). Rainforest soil is relatively infertile, though, with nutrients found only in a shallow surface layer of decaying **organic** matter, which is easily eroded after trees are cleared from the land. Although burning the rainforest vegetation temporarily enriches the soil, it is only a short time before the farmers have to move on to find new land. Large corporate farms growing soybeans, corn, cotton, and rice have also been established on cleared rainforest lands throughout the Amazon, as have huge cattle ranches.

Forests aren't the only plant habitats cleared for agriculture. The rich soil of the world's temperate grasslands has made them a prime target for conversion to cultivation. The steppes of central Europe and the plains of North America have been almost completely cleared of native plants in order to grow crops such as wheat and corn. Grasslands that are too dry to support crops are used as grazing lands for livestock. Even Mediterranean biomes and parts of the world's arid deserts have been converted to grazing land.

Also called "swidden agriculture" or "shifting cultivation," slash-and-burn is a technique practiced by hundreds of millions of people.

## Greener Pastures

Ironically, many rainforest lands are being destroyed in order to grow biofuels, or plant-based sources of energy that are supposed to be better for the environment than burning fossil fuels. Biofuel crops can include sugar cane, palm oil, soybeans, corn, and jatropha trees. Although these plants store carbon, they do not store nearly as much as the trees they are replacing. In fact, when the carbon released into the atmosphere as the result of deforestation to plant biofuels is taken into account, biofuels such as corn ethanol and soy biodiesel produce about twice as much carbon dioxide as gasoline.

Many home gardeners enjoy the beauty of *Tulipa sprengeri* as well as how easy it is to grow, as the plant seeds and spreads on its own.

Plant habitats are also destroyed as human cities expand. The world's temperate and boreal forests have been drastically altered as urban areas, or cities, in the Northern Hemisphere have grown. Although generally located in areas with fewer humans, tropical rainforests are also threatened by development and expansion, especially as roads are cut through forests in order to connect once-remote regions. Mediterranean regions and some deserts, with their warm climates, are also at risk from urban expansion. One of the fastest-growing urban areas in the U.S. is around Phoenix in the Sonoran Desert of Arizona.

Often, habitat destruction is made worse by overexploitation. In less developed regions of the world, for example, the collection of wood for fuel endangers plant communities. In the African country of Niger, 90 percent of household energy is provided by wood, which led to the destruction of more than 1.67 million acres (675,825 ha) of forest from 1990 to 2005. Trees are not the only overexploited plants, though. Beautiful flowers, strange-looking cacti, and exotic carnivorous plants are often plucked from their native habitat to satisfy the desires of plant collectors willing to pay huge sums for rare species. Specimens of *Encephalartos*, a group of African cycads, for example, can sell for thousands of dollars, which has led collectors to harvest so many that fewer than 100 individuals of some species remain in the wild.

Sometimes the threat to plants comes not from what humans have taken out of the natural environment but from what they have introduced into it, in the form of non-native plants. Sometimes these plants are transferred to new locations unintentionally, but in many cases, they have been planted in gardens only to rapidly spread and take over the habitat of native plants. Such harmful non-native plants are referred to as invasive species. Kudzu, a Japanese vine that was planted along American

## Greener Pastures

Home gardens can play an important role in plant conservation. Gardens planted with native species can help to preserve local plant populations while also serving as a home for native wildlife. And the cultivation of rare species can help to stave off extinction of these plants. In fact, many plants that have gone extinct in the wild, such as the tulip species *Tulipa sprengeri*, today thrive in gardens. When purchasing rare species, however, gardeners should be sure to check that the plants have been **propagated** in a nursery and not collected from the wild.

roadways to help prevent erosion, has spread to smother trees, gardens, and small fields across 7 million acres (2.8 million ha) of the southern U.S. Invasive **pathogens** and invasive insects can also wipe out entire plant populations. The American chestnut, a tree that once covered most of eastern North America, was nearly exterminated by chestnut blight, a disease introduced from imported Asian chestnut wood. And the Asian long-horned beetle has bored into and damaged at least 18 tree species in the U.S.

The introduction of pollution into plant habitats can also wreak havoc on plant communities. One of the greatest contributors to pollution is the burning of fossil fuels such as coal and oil. Because many fossil fuels are made up of a number of elements, including sulfur and nitrogen, burning them releases harmful gases such as sulfur dioxide and nitrogen oxide into the atmosphere. There, these gases mix with moisture and fall back to Earth as acid rain, snow, or fog. When this acidic precipitation falls on plants, it damages their leaves and roots, restricts **germination** and reproduction, and often gradually kills them.

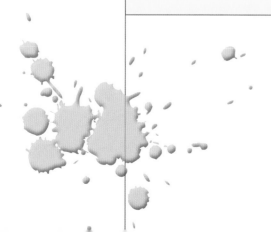

Starting in 2001, Tokyo, Japan, implemented a plan that required certain newly constructed buildings to include green roofs.

## Greener Pastures

In cities around the world, plants are sprouting high in the air, thanks to green roofs. These roofs, which are partially or completely planted with anything from grass to complex plant ecosystems, are especially popular in Germany, where one-tenth of all flat-roofed buildings are green. The roofs are also gaining popularity in central Europe, Japan, Canada, and some U.S. cities, including Chicago. Benefits of green roofs include pollution control, reduced storm water runoff, and climate control, as the plants provide a layer of insulation against extreme heat and cold. In addition, green roofs provide habitat for urban wildlife and can even offer recreational space for humans.

In addition to being planted in vast fields, sunflowers are also grown in cities to reclaim vacant lots and provide ecological services.

## Greener Pastures

Some plants can be used to help restore polluted lands and waters in a process known as phytoremediation. For example, sunflowers are used to remove heavy metals or **radioactive** substances such as uranium from contaminated soil or water. After the plants have absorbed the toxins, they are harvested and safely discarded. (Metal-containing plants are often burned, while radioactive plant material can be **vitrified** and buried in steel canisters.) Other plants break down organic contaminants into harmless compounds. For example, the parrot feather—an invasive freshwater plant—has been used to break down the chemicals in the explosive material TNT at former weapons manufacturing sites in the U.S.

The burning of fossil fuels leads not only to acid rain but also to global warming, which further endangers plant life. Although scientists disagree about the exact causes and extent of global warming, many believe that greenhouse gases such as carbon dioxide could cause Earth's surface temperature to rise by 2 to 11.5 °F (1 to 6.4 °C) over the next century. Such warming could cause plants to flower early, before pollinators such as bees have fully developed. It could also lead to the increased prevalence of harmful insects—such as the spruce bark beetle—that survive more easily and reproduce more quickly in warm climates. As global temperatures warm, the world's climate regions are likely to shift, with warmer temperatures being found closer to the poles or higher up mountains than they are currently. Those plants that require cooler growing conditions may have to shift their range toward the poles (or upward on mountains) as a result. Plants that are already close to mountain summits or that cannot adapt quickly enough may not survive.

Bees play an integral role in the reproduction of some flower species, as they pick up pollen from one flower and deposit it on another.

As the basis of all food chains, plants form the foundation for all other life on Earth. Humans are no exception. We survive by either eating plants directly or eating animals that have eaten plants. Although humans have learned to cultivate domestic crops and no longer rely solely on gathering food from wild plants, wild species still play a role in providing food for human needs.

## CHAPTER THREE

# People and Plants

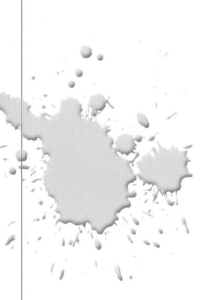

In addition to the fruits, nuts, and berries that wild plants provide directly, they also serve as a store of **genes** that can be used to help improve domestic crops. Today, humans cultivate about 80 different crop plants, relying on only 12—bananas, beans, cassava, corn, millet, potatoes, rice, sorghum, soybeans, sugar cane, sweet potatoes, and wheat—for 75 percent of the total food supply. The failure of any one of these crops could be catastrophic, causing severe famines. Wild plants can help to stave off such failures by providing genes that can be transferred to domestic crops through genetic engineering. Such genes can improve the crops' resistance to pests, speed up their growth rate, or increase their nutritional value. A rare species of wild corn called *Zea diploperennis*, for example, may provide genes that could enable domestic corn to resist several common diseases; when it was discovered, the species was approaching extinction due to habitat loss. Scientists worry that the continued destruction of plant habitat could eliminate other potentially important wild plants before they are even discovered.

Similar concerns plague scientists who make medicines from plants. Today, 80 percent of the population of the **developing world** relies on traditional plant-based medicines. Worldwide, half of all medicinal drugs are derived from plants and contain

In countries such as the U.S., corn is now intentionally grown in abundance to both provide food and be made into many products.

The flowers of a rosy periwinkle are white to dark pink and make it an attractive choice for home gardens in tropical parts of the world.

either natural plant compounds or **synthetic** chemicals based on plant compounds. Aspirin, for example, was originally made from the bark of the willow tree, but it is now produced synthetically. And the cancer-fighting drug paclitaxel was developed from the bark of the Pacific yew tree but is now semi-synthetically produced using yew tree needles. Two other anti-cancer agents, made from the rosy periwinkle, have helped to completely cure many cases of childhood leukemia and Hodgkin's disease. Although the rosy periwinkle is now grown on plantations, it was once in danger of extinction in its native Madagascar. Botanic Gardens Conservation International estimates that another 400 medicinal plants from around the globe are threatened with extinction. And because only one percent of all known plant species has been fully assessed for medicinal properties, there are likely to be many more plants that could yield cures to human ailments—if they don't become extinct first.

A member of the ginger family, turmeric is cultivated for its underground stems, which are used in spices, perfumes, and dyes.

## Greener Pastures

Today, many pharmaceutical companies participate in "bioprospecting," or the search for plant compounds that may provide cures to human ailments. In the past, many of these companies have placed **patents** on the plant compounds that provided such cures, even when the plants were taken from other nations—a practice known as biopiracy. In 1995, for example, two U.S. scientists tried to patent turmeric, a yellow powder made from a plant native to India, where turmeric has been used medicinally for centuries. Today, United Nations guidelines hold that countries should receive payment for access to their plants or royalty payments for products developed from those plants.

Logging in Borneo's rainforests endangers the diverse array of the Southeast Asian island's nearly 3,000 species of trees.

Native women who pick oolong tea leaves in the mountains of northern Thailand contribute to their family's income as well as their country's economy and trade.

Along with food and medicine, plants provide humans with materials such as timber, paper, and clothing. These products are an important part of the global economy. When plants are lost to overexploitation, land conversion, or other causes, it means not only that wood-based products become less available, but also that the people whose livelihoods are dependent upon wood products are threatened with a loss of income. In developing countries, especially, many rural people rely on the collection of wild food, firewood, and medicinal plants as a source of income.

In addition to providing materials for direct human use, plants also help to regulate human surroundings by providing important "ecosystem services." Plants make the air breathable by releasing oxygen during photosynthesis. They also clean the air, filtering pollutants from it. At the same time, plants absorb carbon dioxide, one of the major greenhouse gases contributing to global warming. When plants—especially trees—are destroyed, not only can they no longer absorb carbon dioxide, but most of the carbon that was stored within them is released into the atmosphere as the plants are either burned or decay over time. In fact, deforestation is believed to account for one-fifth of the carbon dioxide released into the atmosphere every year. This means that deforestation emits more carbon dioxide than all the vehicles in the world, making it a significant contributor to global warming.

Deforestation can also affect the planet's climate by changing rainfall patterns. As trees transpire, they release water vapor into the atmosphere that later falls back to Earth as rain. In the Amazon rainforest, for example, half of the 98 to 394 inches (250–1,000 cm) of rain that falls each year comes from plant transpiration. Fewer plants undergoing transpiration means that less water will be released into the atmosphere, so as larger areas of the rainforest are cleared, the climate is likely to

## Greener Pastures

For the most part, the Amazon rainforest is a thick, inaccessible jungle. But more than 100,000 miles (160,935 km) of roads, many of them illegal, have been cut through that jungle, making it easier for loggers, farmers, and ranchers to access—and chop down—once-remote forests. In fact, 85 percent of Amazonian deforestation occurs within 30 miles (48.3 km) of a road. Although many of the roads through the rainforest are little more than dirt tracks that are often impassable, environmentalists are concerned about Brazil's plan to pave the entire 1,110 miles (1,770 km) of the highway BR-163, which passes through nearly a quarter of the rainforest.

Brazil's efforts to decrease deforestation in the Amazon showed in June 2009, as deforestation was down a modest but encouraging 4.4 percent from June 2008.

become drier. Other areas nearby—and even as far away as the U.S.—could also be affected with drier weather as a result of deforestation in the Amazon.

Plants regulate not only water quantity but also water quality. As plants take in water, they often filter harmful compounds out of it, releasing purified vapor back into the atmosphere. By absorbing water and binding soil into place, plants also help to slow water flows and prevent catastrophic floods. In boreal forests, for example, thick stands of tall conifers block spring sunlight from warming the ground too quickly and causing rapid snowmelt. When an area of forest has been clear-cut, spring rains and snowmelt can flow unimpeded across the land, making floods that used to occur once every 100 years into nearly annual events. In addition, when plants are no longer available to shield and bind the soil, excessive rainfall can cause severe erosion. Deadly mudslides can also result; in 2005, Hurricane Stan caused massive mudslides in deforested areas of Guatemala, killing more than 1,000 people.

While people everywhere are affected by the loss of plants, those who live in close contact with natural ecosystems probably face the most immediate threat from plant destruction. Several **indigenous** cultures still live deep within the world's most remote forests, but as loggers and farmers encroach upon their lands, their native ways of life are being lost. In the Central African Republic, the Ba'Aka (also known as Pygmies) have been forced to relocate to settlement camps as their homeland is logged. Often, displaced tribes are unable to sustain their traditional way of life in the face of the modern world, and members of many previously uncontacted tribes succumb to common illnesses such as colds. When these tribes are lost, so is their unique knowledge of the homelands they have known for centuries.

In October 2005, torrential rains linked to the storms produced by
Hurricane Stan caused deadly mudslides in Panabaj, Guatemala.

Many scientists fear that if current trends continue, the world will soon face a plant extinction crisis, with up to a quarter of all flowering plant species—and untold numbers of other plants—becoming extinct over the next few decades. Fortunately, measures have been taken to ensure that the world's plants survive far into the future. In many cases, the first step is to pass laws aimed at protecting plants. In the U.S., for example, the Endangered Species Act prohibits the removal of endangered plants from government-owned lands. And in Brazil, landowners are allowed to remove trees from only 20 percent of their land, although this law can be difficult to enforce. International agreements such as the Convention on International Trade in Endangered Species of Wild Fauna and Flora (CITES) govern the global trade in endangered plants as well.

CHAPTER FOUR

# Planting the Future

In addition to establishing laws to protect specific plant species, governments often set aside areas of plant habitat on which human activity is either forbidden or restricted. Today, more than 102,000 protected areas cover a total of more than 12.5 percent of Earth's land area. Most of these reserves are on islands or in tropical rainforests. The least-protected habitats are temperate grasslands, of which less than five percent are protected, and then only in backyard-sized fragments.

Although protecting plants in the wild is the best way to conserve species, sometimes a plant's habitat is so degraded that it can no longer survive in the wild. Fortunately, many species that have become rare in the wild (as well as many more that continue to thrive) are grown in botanical gardens around the world. Today, many botanical gardens also host seed banks, in

A prairie restoration project adjoins
Chain O Lakes State Park in Illinois,
protecting 3,230 acres (1,307 ha)
of native grasslands.

## Greener Pastures

London's Kew Gardens feature the world's largest and most diverse collection of live plants. The botanical gardens' herbarium, or collection of preserved specimens, holds millions more. Founded in 1759, Kew today employs 700 staff members, including 200 scientists and 200 **horticulturists.** Staff members focus not only on growing and researching plants at the gardens but also on preserving wild plants around the world through collaborations with institutions in other countries. In addition, Kew Gardens hosts the storage facility for the Millennium Seed Bank Project, preserving more than a billion seeds that represent nearly 10 percent of all plant species on Earth.

Visitors to Kew Gardens can roam through the flowerbeds, hop on the Kew Explorer for a 40-minute tour, or attend classes and lectures.

which thousands of plant seeds are preserved in below-freezing temperatures to serve as backups to live plant populations. For those plants that are unable to reproduce naturally, botanical gardens have experimented with techniques of micropropagation, in which a new plant is grown from small pieces of plant tissue. The Australian plant Corrigin grevillea, for example, was once thought to be extinct in the wild, but micropropagation allowed hundreds of plants to be grown at botanical gardens, and they were eventually reintroduced into the wild.

Sometimes not only individual plant species but entire plant ecosystems are the focus of restoration efforts. In some cases, abandoned farmland will reforest naturally, which happened across the eastern U.S. as people moved to cities during much of the 20th century. In other places, conservationists have replanted trees and grasses on formerly logged or farmed land. Restoration efforts often require intense management, however, and are ultimately much more expensive than preventing ecosystems from being destroyed in the first place.

Forests dominated by beech trees thrive throughout the landscape of southern England and have stood there for centuries.

In order to protect the world's remaining natural forest eco-systems, which are known as old-growth forests, some scientists have called for a ban on all old-growth logging. They contend that the trees needed for timber products should be grown on tree farms planted on land that has already been converted. Indeed, many tree plantations around the world already grow single tree species—usually conifers or eucalyptus—for the purpose of harvesting their wood. Although these monocultures (stands of single tree species) are typically unsuitable habitats for other forest plants and animals, proponents say that if such plantations prevent the logging of the world's remaining natural forests, they will ultimately save many forest dwellers.

The more than 500 known species of eucalyptus trees are all native to Australia, New Zealand, Tasmania, and nearby islands.

Others argue that rather than restricting logging to tree farms, natural forests should be logged selectively and sustainably. In selective logging, specific trees are carefully removed from forests, and new trees are planted in their place. In parts of Brazil, for example, foresters carefully identify and map each tree to be logged, selecting only a few of each species at a time. They then carefully remove the trees from the forest, making sure not to disturb surrounding trees and plants. In addition, each section of forest is logged only once every 30 years. Loggers who follow such selective practices are often certified by the Forest Stewardship Council (an international nonprofit organization) as producing products that are sustainably managed.

In order to preserve other wild plants, some conservationists have focused on providing **incentives** to landowners; if landowners feel that they can make more money by leaving natural plants in place than by clearing them for timber or agriculture, they will be more likely to preserve plant populations. In Brazil, for example, harvesting Brazil nuts brings long-term income to rural landholders, and in the Petén region of Guatemala, local families earn an average annual income of nearly $1,000 each through the sustainable extraction of rainforest products. In other places, agriculture is carried out within forests in a practice known as agroforestry. Coffee and tea, which can be grown in shade, are often planted beneath natural rainforest trees, for example.

Other conservation incentive programs have gone even further. In 2008, the United Nations (UN) established the UN Collaborative Programme on Reduced Emissions from Deforestation and Forest Degradation in Developing Countries (UN-REDD). As part of the program, voluntary donors pay developing countries for reducing their emissions of greenhouse gases from deforestation. The payments are meant to help offset the revenue that could have been earned

Collecting Brazil nuts first entails picking up the 4-pound (2 kg) fruit
of the Brazil nut tree, which contains 8 to 24 seeds—the "nuts."

by logging the trees. In the future, countries that lower their deforestation rates may also be able to sell "carbon credits" to **developed countries** that are unable to lower their greenhouse gas emissions below a certain level.

In 2002, the governing body of the Convention on Biological Diversity (an international treaty created to preserve biodiversity) adopted the Global Strategy for Plant Conservation. The strategy aims by 2010 to, among other things, assess the conservation status of all known plant species, conserve at least 10 percent of each of the world's ecological regions, and ensure that 30 percent of plant-based products come from sustainable sources. As of 2009, progress toward meeting many of these goals appeared to be mixed, but the strategy had succeeded in spurring a number of new plant conservation initiatives. Fortunately, people around the world have recognized that Earth stands at the brink of a plant extinction crisis—and they are working to make the planet green again.

After paper is taken to a waste collection plant, all the ink that was printed on it is removed so the paper can be recycled further.

## Greener Pastures

You can play a role in helping to conserve trees by using wood products responsibly. Use recycled wood for building, and do not buy furniture made from woods such as mahogany or teak (unless it has been certified by the Forest Stewardship Council or the Rainforest Alliance). Look for products with a minimum of paper or cardboard packaging, and try to avoid using paper plates, napkins, and cups. Whenever possible, purchase recycled paper, and be sure to recycle whatever paper you use. The production of 1 ton (0.9 t) of recycled paper saves 17 trees from being harvested.

## Greener Pastures

Today, more than 250 million acres (101 million ha) around the world are planted with genetically engineered, or genetically modified (GM), crops. Some environmentalists hail GM crops because the plants' natural ability to resist pests means that they need fewer toxic substances applied to them. GM crops also enable farmers to produce more food per acre (0.4 ha). Some fear, however, that GM plants could crossbreed with their wild relatives, transferring their genes to wild plants and reducing biodiversity. Others fear that GM foods could adversely affect human health, although GM crops have so far proven to be safe.

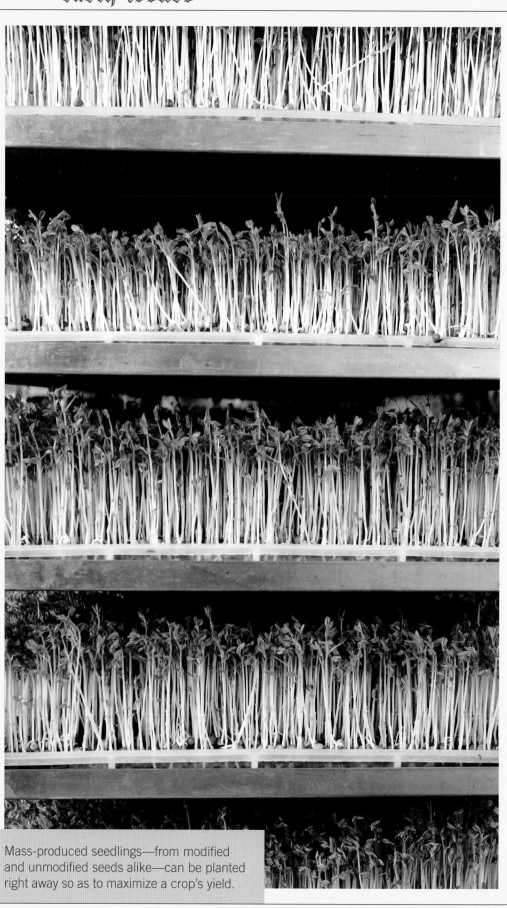

Mass-produced seedlings—from modified and unmodified seeds alike—can be planted right away so as to maximize a crop's yield.

# Glossary

**atmosphere**—the layer of gases that surrounds Earth

**biodiversity**—the variety of life in the world or in a certain habitat

**biomes**—natural communities of plants and animals occupying a major habitat defined by a specific climate

**boreal**—of the northern part of the world; characteristic of the cold region south of the Arctic that features forests of conifers and other trees such as birch and poplar

**deciduous**—leaf-shedding; deciduous trees and shrubs lose their leaves in the fall

**developed countries**—the wealthier nations of the world, which are generally characterized by high individual incomes, along with high levels of education and industrialization

**developing world**—having to do with the poorest countries of the world, which are generally characterized by a lack of health care, nutrition, education, and industry; most developing countries are in Africa, Asia, and Latin America

**ecosystems**—communities of organisms that depend on one another and interact with their environment

**genes**—the basic units of heredity that transmit traits or characteristics from parents to offspring

**germination**—the process by which plants begin to sprout or grow

**hardwoods**—broad-leaved, usually deciduous, trees, as opposed to conifers

**horticulturists**—people who cultivate and manage gardens or conduct research on plants

**incentives**—things, such as money, that motivate people to take specific actions

**indigenous**—originating in a particular place

**mammals**—warm-blooded, hairy animals that have a backbone and feed their young with milk from the mother's body

**molecules**—the smallest units of a substance that retain the characteristics of that substance; molecules are made up of one or more atoms

**organic**—derived from or relating to living matter

**overexploitation**—the excessive use of a resource to the point of causing it to almost disappear

**patents**—legal documents granting inventors the sole right to make or sell their inventions

**pathogens**—disease-causing agents, such as bacteria or viruses

**pigment**—a material or substance present in the tissues of animals or plants that gives them their natural coloring

**propagated**—bred from seeds or cuttings

**radioactive**—characteristic of substances such as uranium that give off particles of energy as their atoms decay; the energy is dangerous to human health

**subsistence farmers**—people who farm to provide enough food to feed their family, with little or no product left over to sell

**succulents**—plants such as cacti and aloes that have thick, fleshy leaves or stems for storing water

**synthetic**—made artificially through chemical processes, especially to imitate a natural product

**temperate**—denoting a region or climate marked by moderate or mild temperatures

**vitrified**—converted into glass

# Bibliography

Chivian, Eric, and Aaron Bernstein, eds. *Sustaining Life: How Human Health Depends on Biodiversity*. New York: Oxford University Press, 2008.

Eldredge, Niles. *Life in the Balance: Humanity and the Biodiversity Crisis*. Princeton, N.J.: Princeton University Press, 1998.

Jensen, Derrick, and George Draffan. *Strangely Like War: The Global Assault on Forests*. White River Junction, Vt.: Chelsea Green Publishing, 2003.

London, Mark, and Brian Kelly. *The Last Forest: The Amazon in the Age of Globalization*. New York: Random House, 2007.

Marinelli, Janet, ed. *Plant*. New York: DK Publishing, 2005.

Savage, Candace. *Prairie: A Natural History*. Vancouver: Greystone Books, 2004.

Tudge, Colin. *The Tree*. New York: Crown Publishers, 2006.

Wilson, Edward O. *The Future of Life*. New York: Alfred A. Knopf, 2002.

# For Further Information

## Books

Ballard, Carol. *The Search for Cures from the Rain Forest*.
Milwaukee: Gareth Stevens Publishing, 2005.

Collard, Sneed B. *The Prairie Builders: Reconstructing America's Lost Grasslands*.
Boston: Houghton Mifflin, 2005.

Souza, D. M. *Endangered Plants*. New York: Franklin Watts, 2003.

Welsbacher, Anne. *Protecting Earth's Rain Forests*.
Minneapolis: Lerner Publications, 2009.

## Web Sites

University of Illinois Urban Programs: The Great Plant Escape
http://www.urbanext.uiuc.edu/gpe/index.html

Missouri Botanical Garden: What's It Like Where You Live?
http://www.mbgnet.net/sets/index.htm

Rainforest Action Network: Rainforest Heroes
http://www.ran.org/new/kidscorner/home

United States Botanic Garden Kids Page
http://www.usbg.gov/forkids.cfm

# Index